Vocabulary Activities

Level 3

Columbus, OH

The **McGraw·Hill** Companies

SRAonline.com

 SRA

Send all inquiries to:
SRA/McGraw-Hill
8787 Orion Place
Columbus, OH 43240-4027

ISBN 0-07-604121-2

1 2 3 4 5 6 7 8 9 BCH 11 10 09 08 07 06 05

The *McGraw·Hill* Companies

Table of Contents

Vocabulary Activities

Level 3

Activity 1

> **tease** (p. 14) To annoy continuously
> **van** (p. 15) A big truck
> **seriously** (p. 16) Thoughtfully
> **practice** (p. 16) Do again and again to gain skill
>
> **collection** (p. 18) Similar things gathered together
> **kite** (p. 19) A flying toy
> **heavily** (p. 23) Strongly
> **stiff** (p. 24) Not easily bent
> **drew** (p. 25) Pulled
> **probably** (p. 25) Most likely

Fill in each blank with a vocabulary word from this lesson to complete each sentence.

1. Holden _____ the door closed.

2. Becca worked _____ on her homework.

3. My mom _____ will drive the _____ tonight.

4. Mr. Simmons snored _____ in his chair.

5. We used _____ paper to make birthday cards.

6. I _____ my multiplication facts every day.

7. Don't _____ your little sister!

8. Hannah has a _____ of stuffed animals.

UNIT 1 Friendship • **Lesson** 1 *Gloria Who Might Be My Best Friend*

Activity 2

drew	seriously	kite	stiff	tease
collection	probably	heavily	van	practice

Write the word from the word box that matches each definition below.

1. _____ do again and again to gain skill

2. _____ a big truck

3. _____ thoughtfully

4. _____ similar things gathered together

5. _____ strongly

6. _____ not easily bent

7. _____ pulled

8. _____ a flying toy

9. _____ to annoy continuously

10. _____ most likely

UNIT I Friendship • **Lesson 2** *Angel Child, Dragon Child*

Activity 3

---

tilted (p. 28) Past tense of **tilt:** to tip

traced (p. 31) Past tense of **trace:** to copy by following lines seen through thin paper

gleamed (p. 33) Past tense of **gleam:** to shine

darted (p. 35) Past tense of **dart:** to move suddenly and quickly

whined (p. 37) Past tense of **whine:** to talk in a complaining voice

blurred (p. 37) Past tense of **blur:** to become hard to see

scrawled (p. 40) Past tense of **scrawl:** to write quickly but not carefully

margins (p. 40) Plural of **margin:** an empty space at the edge of the paper

fair (p. 41) A show or exhibition

Review the vocabulary words and definitions from *Angel Child, Dragon Child*. Write two sentences that each use at least one of the vocabulary words from this lesson.

1. _____

   _____

2. _____

   _____

Activity 4

Tell whether the boldfaced definition that is given for the underlined word in each sentence below makes sense. Circle Yes or No.

1. Petra <u>whined</u> about the rain.
   talked in a complaining voice .... Yes   No

2. We rode the Ferris wheel at the <u>fair</u>.
   a show or exhibition .... Yes   No

3. Fog <u>blurred</u> the outline of the houses.
   tipped .... Yes   No

4. Luis drew animals in the <u>margins</u> of the letter.
   empty spaces at the edge of the paper .... Yes   No

5. The rabbit <u>darted</u> into the bushes.
   moved suddenly and quickly .... Yes   No

6. I <u>traced</u> the flower from the library book.
   wrote quickly but not carefully .... Yes   No

7. Who <u>tilted</u> the milk jug and made the mess?
   tipped .... Yes   No

8. The snow <u>gleamed</u> in the sunlight.
   became hard to see .... Yes   No

9. The teacher <u>scrawled</u> a note to my parents.
   wrote quickly but not carefully .... Yes   No

Activity 5

> **terrific** (p. 48) Great
> **magnificent** (p. 48) Outstanding
> **hinges** (p. 48) Plural of **hinge:** a metal joint that attaches a door to its frame
> **peered** (p. 51) Past tense of **peer:** to look
> **prop** (p. 51) To lean
> **trunk** (p. 51) The main stem of a tree
>
> **borrow** (p. 54) To receive something with the understanding that it must be given back
> **height** (p. 57) How tall something is
> **curtains** (p. 58) Plural of **curtain:** a hanging for a window
> **portraits** (p. 58) Plural of **portrait:** a picture of someone

Circle the correct word that completes each sentence.

1. The _____ squeaked when Larissa came in.
   a. kites   b. curtains   c. hinges

2. Elliot _____ into the basement.
   a. scrawled   b. peered   c. gleamed

3. Don't _____ the glass there!
   a. practice   b. borrow   c. prop

4. The choir sounds _____ .
   a. magnificent   b. heavily   c. stiff

5. Jim's dad paints _____ of sports stars.
   a. hinges   b. portraits   c. curtains

UNIT 1 Friendship • **Lesson 3** *The Tree House*

▶ Activity 6

Match each word on the left to its definition on the right.

1. borrow   **a.** to lean

2. curtains   **b.** pictures of someone

3. terrific   **c.** to receive something with the
                                understanding that it must be
                                given back

4. prop   **d.** how tall something is

5. portraits   **e.** the main stem of a tree

6. height   **f.** outstanding

7. hinges   **g.** great

8. magnificent   **h.** metal joints that attach a door
                                to its frame

9. peered   **i.** hangings for windows

10. trunk   **j.** looked

Activity 7

---

chores (p. 64) Plural of **chore:** a small job

patient (p. 66) Willing to wait

bother (p. 67) To annoy

ignore (p. 67) To pay no attention to

worried (p. 68) Past tense of **worry:** to think about troubles

energy (p. 70) The capacity for vigorous activities

especially (p. 76) Particularly

permission (p. 76) Consent that allows one to do something

grateful (p. 78) Thankful

nervous (p. 79) Uneasy

Circle the word in parentheses that best fits each sentence.

1. Mei has more (portraits/energy) on the weekend.

2. I am (grateful/patient) to have a smart teacher.

3. Sally is (stiff/nervous) during storms.

4. Nate is (ignore/patient) with his sister.

5. My mom gave me (permission/energy) to go on the trip.

6. Don't (ignore/grateful) me when I am talking!

7. Suki is (patient/worried) about her sick dog.

8. I have to do (chores/energy) every Saturday.

Name _____ Date _____

grateful	energy	ignore	patient	nervous
permission	chores	worried	bother	especially

Write the word from the word box that best matches the underlined word or phrase in the sentences below.

1. I am <u>willing to wait</u> when my mom is late. _____

2. Wade and Ely <u>annoy</u> the rest of the class. _____

3. The girls <u>pay no attention</u> to the barking dogs. _____

4. Sheryl asked her mom for <u>consent to do something</u>.

   _____

5. Puppies have lots of <u>capacity for vigorous activities</u>.

   _____

6. We were <u>particularly</u> hungry this morning. _____

7. Ty <u>thought about troubles</u> about finishing his homework.

   _____

8. Amira is <u>thankful</u> that the family is together. _____

9. I do many <u>small jobs</u> on the weekend. _____

10. Lance feels <u>uneasy</u> about the big game. _____

Activity 9

---

leagues (p. 83) Plural of
  league: a group of teams
challenge (p. 85) To question
  the truth of
compete (p. 85) To try to win
treated (p. 85) Past tense of
  treat: to act in a specified
  manner toward someone
possess (p. 86) To have
opponents (p. 86) Plural of
  opponent: a person on the
  other side

series (p. 87) Several in a row
organizations (p. 87) The
  plural of **organization**: a
  group of people who join
  together for a purpose
responded (p. 89) Past tense of
  respond: to answer
equal (p. 90) The same as

Circle the correct word that completes each sentence.

1. Toshiro and Laura have an _____ number of books.
   a. equal   b. opponent   c. especially

2. We will _____ for the top prize.
   a. challenge   b. borrow   c. compete

3. Fernando _____ to the phone call.
   a. responded   b. treated   c. possess

4. His _____ ran faster in the game.
   a. series   b. leagues   c. opponents

5. My dad belongs to many _____ .
   a. opponents   b. chores   c. organizations

Name _____ Date _____

Activity 10

| leagues | equal | opponents | organizations | series |
| treated | challenge | responded | compete | possess |

Write the word from the word box that matches each definition below.

1. _____ to question the truth of

2. _____ to have

3. _____ groups of people who join together for a purpose

4. _____ the same as

5. _____ acted in a specified manner toward someone

6. _____ several in a row

7. _____ to try to win

8. _____ groups of teams

9. _____ answered

10. _____ people on the other side

UNIT I Friendship • **Lesson 6** *The Legend of Damon and Pythias*

Activity II

---

rule (p. 97) To have control over

persuaded (p. 99) Past tense of **persuade**: to convince

certain (p. 101) Sure

curious (p. 102) Interested in knowing

exchange (p. 102) To trade

condition (p. 103) Something required

deserted (p. 105) Past tense of **desert**: to leave alone

struggled (p. 107) Past tense of **struggle**: to make a great effort

faith (p. 108) Confidence

miserable: (p. 108) Very unhappy

**Review the vocabulary words and definitions
from *The Legend of Damon and Pythias*.
Write two sentences that each use at least
one of the vocabulary words from this lesson.**

1. _____

   _____

2. _____

   _____

UNIT 1 Friendship • **Lesson 6** *The Legend of Damon and Pythias*

Activity 12

Tell whether the boldfaced definition that is given for the underlined word in each sentence below makes sense. Circle Yes or No.

1. Kim persuaded me to go skiing.
   convinced .... Yes No

2. The king and queen rule the whole country.
   to make a great effort .... Yes No

3. The team felt miserable after losing the game.
   very unhappy .... Yes No

4. Jared and Adam exchange lunch every day.
   to leave alone .... Yes No

5. The team deserted Skye in the dark gym.
   to have control over .... Yes No

6. We will go fishing tomorrow with the condition it does not rain. **something required** .... Yes No

7. I am certain we will win the race.
   sure .... Yes No

8. Johanna struggled with her homework.
   traded .... Yes No

9. We have faith in our principal.
   confidence .... Yes No

10. The curious kitten looked out the bedroom window. **interested in knowing** .... Yes No

UNIT I   Friendship • Review

Unit I Review

Circle the correct word that completes each sentence.

1. Colby has a _____ of toy cars.
   a. collection   b. portrait   c. practice

2. Stephanie leaned on the _____ of the oak tree.
   a. height   b. hinges   c. trunk

3. Claire is a _____ babysitter.
   a. stiff   b. terrific   c. curious

4. The boys are all tall, _____ Marcus.
   a. seriously   b. especially   c. probably

5. I have to finish my _____ before I can play.
   a. chores   b. practice   c. leagues

6. Don't _____ me while I am doing my homework.
   a. ignore   b. bother   c. challenge

7. We have blue _____ in the kitchen.
   a. hinges   b. margins   c. curtains

8. The _____ of the hoop is ten feet.
   a. height   b. collection   c. trunk

9. Vic likes to fly a _____ on windy days.
   a. fair   b. trunk   c. kite

10. The teams in the baseball _____ will play in a tournament.
    a. leagues   b. series   c. opponents

Name _____ Date _____

Unit I Review

Match each word on the left to its definition on the right.

1. tease   **a.** to pay no attention to

2. ignore   **b.** acted in a specified manner toward someone

3. possess   **c.** very unhappy

4. treated   **d.** to annoy continuously

5. challenge   **e.** made a great effort

6. miserable   **f.** wrote quickly but not carefully

7. darted   **g.** to have

8. persuaded   **h.** to question the truth of

9. struggled   **i.** convinced

10. scrawled   **j.** moved suddenly and quickly

Activity 13

> **spring** (p. 114) The season between winter and summer
> **shades** (p. 115) Sunglasses
> **crops** (p. 115) Plural of **crop:** a plant grown for food or to sell to make money
>
> **decorated** (p. 119) Past tense of **decorate:** to make pretty
> **vacant** (p. 119) Empty
> **mound** (p. 120) A pile of something
> **patch** (p. 121) A small area

Fill in each blank with a vocabulary word from this lesson to complete each sentence.

1. Rex wears cool _____ in the sun.

2. We were scared in the _____, old house.

3. Kamila _____ her bedroom with colored lights.

4. The Millers planted _____ in the _____ of land behind the barn.

5. Terrell has a _____ of dirty socks.

6. _____ is my favorite season.

UNIT 2 City Wildlife • **Lesson I** *The Boy Who Didn't Believe in Spring*

Activity 14

**Match each word on the left to its definition
on the right.**

1. decorated

a. empty

2. patch

b. a pile of something

3. vacant

c. plants grown for food or
to sell to make money

4. shades

d. made pretty

5. mound

e. sunglasses

6. spring

f. the season between
winter and summer

7. crops

g. a small area

Name _____   Date _____

Activity 15

> **cliffs** (p. 127) Plural of **cliff:** a high, steep face of rock
>
> **thought** (p. 127) Past tense of **think:** to believe
>
> **avoid** (p. 128) To keep away from
>
> **concerned** (p. 128) Past tense of **concern:** to worry
>
> **waste** (p. 128) Trash
>
> **affected** (p. 128) Past tense of **affect:** to have an influence on
>
> **rare** (p. 129) Not common
>
> **survive** (p. 129) To stay alive
>
> **designed** (p. 130) Past tense of **design:** to create for a particular purpose
>
> **developments** (p. 130) Plural of **development:** an area of new buildings

Review the vocabulary words and definitions from *City Critters*. Write two sentences that each use at least one of the vocabulary words from this lesson.

1. _____

   _____

2. _____

   _____

Activity 16

developments	waste	thought	rare	survive
cliffs	affected	concerned	designed	avoid

Write the word from the word box that matches each definition below.

1. _____ had an influence on

2. _____ worried

3. _____ believed

4. _____ areas of new buildings

5. _____ to stay alive

6. _____ not common

7. _____ trash

8. _____ created for a particular purpose

9. _____ to keep away from

10. _____ high, steep faces of rocks

Activity 17

> **pond** (p. 136) A small lake
> **enormous** (p. 137) Very big
> **strange** (p. 137) Unusual
> **suited** (p. 137) Past tense of
>   **suit:** to meet the needs of
> **hatch** (p. 138) To come out of
>   an egg
> **cozy** (p. 139) Warm and
>   comfortable
>
> **settled down** (p. 139) Past
>   tense of **settle down:** to
>   make one's home
> **responsibility** (p. 140) A duty
> **bringing up** (p. 140) Raising
>   children
> **beckoned** (p. 142) Past tense
>   of **beckon:** to call someone
>   by waving

Tell whether the boldfaced definition that is given for the underlined word in each sentence below makes sense. Circle Yes or No.

1. Alice reads in a cozy chair.
   warm and comfortable .... Yes   No

2. Marco swims in the pond in the summer.
   a small lake .... Yes   No

3. Hannah beckoned the bus driver.
   to meet the needs of .... Yes   No

4. The turtles hatch on the beach.
   to come out of an egg .... Yes   No

5. You have a responsibility to wash the car.
   unusual .... Yes   No

UNIT 2 City Wildlife • **Lesson 3** *Make Way for Ducklings*

Activity 18

Circle the correct word that completes each sentence.

1. All of the kids rode in the _____ bus.
   a. strange   b. vacant   c. enormous

2. The warm, blue coat _____ Denise.
   a. suited   b. affected   c. designed

3. Haden _____ after he got a job.
   a. thought   b. beckoned   c. settled down

4. I _____ my mother from the window.
   a. decorated   b. beckoned   c. suited

5. Did you see the _____ painting at the museum?
   a. cozy   b. strange   c. vacant

6. The _____ was frozen.
   a. pond   b. cliff   c. mound

7. When will the eggs _____?
   a. hatch   b. settle down   c. survive

8. Our parents are _____ four kids.
   a. concerned   b. suited   c. bringing up

9. Pilar has a _____ to walk the dog.
   a. responsibility   b. pond   c. patch

10. We are _____ by the fire.
    a. strange   b. cozy   c. enormous

Activity 19

---

stirring (p. 148) Moving
explore (p. 149) To search
platform (p. 150) A raised floor
developed (p. 150) Past tense
of **develop**: to grow
surrounds (p. 153) To be on all
sides of
huddle (p. 155) To crowd
together

sweeping (p. 156) Carrying
away
prey (p. 159) An animal that is
hunted by another animal for
food
underneath (p. 160) Below
fascinated (p. 161) Past tense
of **fascinate**: to hold the
interest of

**Circle the word in parentheses that best fits
each sentence.**

1. We waited on the (cliffs/platform) for the bus.

2. I hid (underneath/cozy) the blanket.

3. The story (developed/fascinated) the whole class.

4. The forest (surrounds/huddles) our house.

5. The wind is (bringing up/sweeping) away the snow.

6. The animals (explore/huddle) to stay warm.

7. Emma painted a (sweeping/stirring) picture of her mom.

8. Taylor and Zach went to (explore/huddle) the vacant house.

UNIT 2 City Wildlife • **Lesson 4** *Urban Roosts*

Activity 20

surrounds	explore	fascinated	stirring	sweeping
prey	underneath	huddle	platform	developed

Write the word from the word box that best matches the underlined word or phrase in the sentences below.

1. The <u>moving</u> music made Madison cry. _____

2. The book is <u>below</u> the bed. _____

3. The young pigeons <u>grew</u> adult feathers. _____

4. The choir stood on the <u>raised floor</u>. _____

5. We like to <u>search</u> the woods in the summer.

   _____

6. The players <u>crowd together</u> on the field. _____

7. The water is <u>carrying</u> away the mud. _____

8. The lion chased her <u>animal that is hunted for food</u>

   into the trees. _____

9. Dylan <u>held the interest of</u> the baby with his song.

   _____

10. A fence <u>is on all sides of</u> our yard. _____

Activity 21

> **relocates** (p. 172) Moves to a different place
> **stranded** (p. 172) Past tense of **strand:** to leave in a helpless position
> **announced** (p. 172) Past tense of **announce:** to make known
> **exclaimed** (p. 173) Past tense of **exclaim:** to speak out
> **sharp** (p. 173) Alert
>
> **detect** (p. 173) To find out
> **cautiously** (p. 173) With close care
> **intelligent** (p. 173) Having the ability to learn
> **appreciate** (p. 173) To understand the nature of
> **extended** (p. 178) Past tense of **extend:** to reach out

**Fill in each blank with a vocabulary word
from this lesson to complete each sentence.**

1. The _____ cat moved _____ toward the mouse.

2. "My bicycle is missing!" _____ Paige.

3. Emilio _____ his hand toward Mick.

4. Ms. Ford _____ the time of the test.

5. Heather was _____ when her car broke down.

6. I _____ your loyal friendship.

7. The _____ girl got a perfect score on her test.

UNIT 2 City Wildlife • **Lesson 5** *Two Days in May*

Activity 22

announced	detect	exclaimed	sharp	intelligent
cautiously	appreciate	stranded	extended	relocates

Write the word from the word box that matches each definition below.

1. _____ reached out

2. _____ left in a helpless position

3. _____ with close care

4. _____ made known

5. _____ to understand the nature of

6. _____ to find out

7. _____ moves to a different place

8. _____ alert

9. _____ spoke out

10. _____ having the ability to learn

Activity 23

---

freight (p. 182) Products that are transported by trains, boats, or planes

warehouses (p. 182) Plural of **warehouse:** a building where products are stored

shallow (p. 182) Not deep

concrete (p. 182) A strong building material that hardens as it dries

cling (p. 182) To stick together

slopes (p. 182) Plural of **slope:** an upward or downward slant

binoculars (p. 187) A device to help see objects that are far away

coyote (p. 189) A North American animal that looks like a small, thin wolf

wilderness (p. 190) A wild, natural area that has not been developed by people

rocked (p. 191) Past tense of **rock:** to move back and forth

---

Review the vocabulary words and definitions from *Secret Place*. Write two sentences that each use at least one of the vocabulary words from this lesson.

1. _____

   _____

2. _____

   _____

Name _____ Date _____

Activity 24

Match each word on the left to its definition on the right.

1. warehouses

2. binoculars

3. concrete

4. rocked

5. wilderness

6. cling

7. freight

8. slopes

9. coyote

10. shallow

a. moved back and forth

b. not deep

c. buildings where products are stored

d. a North American animal that looks like a small, thin wolf

e. upward or downward slants

f. a strong building material that hardens as it dries

g. a device to help see objects that are far away

h. to stick together

i. a wild, natural area that has not been developed by people

j. products that are transported by trains, boats, or planes

Unit 2 Review

Circle the word in parentheses that best fits each sentence.

1. We took a back road to (explore/**avoid**) the highway traffic.

2. Sierra (developed/**rocked**) her baby to sleep.

3. The children played in the (**shallow**/strange) pool.

4. Jared's cough (fascinated/**concerned**) his parents.

5. Tamara (**thought**/suited) she saw a deer run into the woods.

6. The mechanic tried to (**detect**/relocate) the problem with the car.

7. The (enormous/**intelligent**) students studied hard for the science test.

8. The workers poured the (freight/**concrete**) for the new sidewalk.

9. Coyotes live in the (warehouses/**wilderness**).

10. The art museum (**fascinated**/concerned) the students.

Name _____ Date _____

Unit 2 Review

affected	settled down	enormous	strange	developed
suited	prey	explore	huddle	relocates

**Write the word from the word box that
matches each definition below.**

1. _____ made one's home

2. _____ to move to a different place

3. _____ to search

4. _____ unusual

5. _____ grew

6. _____ very big

7. _____ had an influence on

8. _____ an animal that is hunted by another animal
for food

9. _____ met the needs of

10. _____ to crowd together

Activity 25

---

carved (p. 198) Past tense of **carve:** to cut carefully
protest (p. 201) To disagree
piece (p. 203) A work of music
imitating (p. 204) Copying
splinters (p. 204) Plural of **splinter:** a small sharp piece of wood broken off from a larger piece

gutter (p. 205) A pipe that carries rainwater
sculpture (p. 205) A figure, statue, or design carved out of something solid
gleam (p. 206) To shine
promptly (p. 207) Quickly
sternly (p. 211) In a strict or harsh way

Write the vocabulary word from this lesson that best matches the underlined word or phrase in the sentences below.

1. The lights <u>shine</u> on the wet street. _____

2. Xavier <u>quickly</u> walked to answer the door. _____

3. The players <u>disagree</u> when the coach ends practice.

    _____

4. Omar played a hard <u>work of music</u> for the concert.

    _____

5. The nurse talked <u>in a strict way</u> to the girls. _____

sternly	splinters	carved	sculpture	imitating
gutter	promptly	gleam	piece	protest

Write the word from the word box to complete each sentence.

1. We _____ when the teacher gives homework.

2. Seth likes the _____ I played last night.

3. Zoey _____ a wooden _____ in the yard.

4. Watch out for _____ on that board!

5. Lisa is _____ my accent.

6. My mother called _____ , and I answered

_____ .

7. We need to clean the leaves out of the _____ .

8. The new cars _____ in the sunshine.

Activity 27

---

poet (p. 216) A person who writes poems

alarm (p. 217) Sudden fear

temperature (p. 218) The hotness or coldness of a thing

commanded (p. 218) Past tense of **command:** to demand

case (p. 219) A set of circumstances

boxed (p. 219) Past tense of **box:** to hit with the fist

colonel (p. 220) An officer in the army, marines, or air force

peacefulness (p. 220) Quiet and calm

praise (p. 221) To speak well of

straight away (p. 221) Right now

Circle the word in parentheses that best fits each sentence.

1. The (colonel/poet) read poems to the class.

2. Caitlyn (commanded/boxed) me to come home.

3. The (temperature/alarm) of the water was warm.

4. Gia's parents (praise/protest) her dancing.

5. Frank likes the (praise/peacefulness) of the ocean.

6. The loud thunder filled the child with (case/alarm).

7. Bring your umbrella in (case/praise) it rains.

8. "Come home (straight away/sternly)," said Dad.

UNIT 3 Imagination • **Lesson 2** *The Cat Who Became a Poet*

Activity 28

**Match each word on the left to its definition
on the right.**

1. temperature

2. straight away

3. praise

4. alarm

5. boxed

6. case

7. commanded

8. colonel

9. peacefulness

10. poet

a. hit with the fist

b. the hotness or coldness of
a thing

c. demanded

d. an officer in the army,
marines, or air force

e. right now

f. sudden fear

g. to speak well of

h. a set of circumstances

i. a person who writes poems

j. quiet and calm

Activity 29

> **fabric** (p. 224) Material used to make clothing
>
> **ordered** (p. 226) Past tense of **order:** to ask for
>
> **design** (p. 226) A plan for putting something together
>
> **pattern** (p. 227) The way in which things are placed
>
> **stitched** (p. 228) Past tense of **stitch:** to sew
>
> **sturdy** (p. 228) Strong
>
> **spare** (p. 228) An extra
>
> **diagonal** (p. 228) A line connecting two opposite angles on a four-sided shape
>
> **proper** (p. 229) Acceptable
>
> **practical** (p. 233) Useful

Review the vocabulary words and definitions from *A Cloak for the Dreamer*. Write two sentences that each use at least one of the vocabulary words from this lesson.

1. _____

_____

2. _____

_____

Name _____ Date _____

Tell whether the boldfaced definition that is given for the underlined word in each sentence below makes sense. Circle Yes or No.

1. Chita <u>ordered</u> a large pizza.
   asked for.. Yes   No

2. Steve has a <u>design</u> for the new playground.
   material used to make clothing .... Yes   No

3. Mom bought purple <u>fabric</u> for the dress.
   the way in which things are placed..................... Yes   No

4. I carry the books in a <u>sturdy</u> box.
   strong .... Yes   No

5. Darryl's dad <u>stitched</u> the rip in his coat.
   asked for.. Yes   No

6. Do you have a <u>spare</u> apple?
   extra .... Yes   No

7. His shirt was not <u>proper</u> for the party.
   acceptable .... Yes   No

8. Linda drew a <u>diagonal</u> line on her paper.
   a plan for putting something together .... Yes   No

9. The wallpaper in our kitchen has a flower <u>pattern</u>.
   the way in which things are placed..................... Yes   No

10. Tools are <u>practical</u> gifts for Mom.
    useful... Yes   No

Activity 31

---

local (p. 240) In a nearby place

encouraged (p. 240) Past tense of **encourage:** to urge someone to do something

style (p. 240) The way something is done

period (p. 240) A portion of time

mood (p. 242) A general state of mind

series (p. 245) Several in a row

monuments (p. 245) Plural of **monument:** something built to honor a person or event

originality (p. 246) Newness

imagination (p. 246) The ability to create new ideas in one's mind

biography (p. 247) A true story of someone's life written by another person

---

Circle the correct word that completes each sentence.

1. Wes had a _____ of tests this week.
   a. pattern   b. design   c. series

2. The teacher loved the _____ of the design.
   a. originality   b. local   c. case

3. Tara wrote a _____ of her father for school.
   a. sculpture   b. monument   c. biography

4. Grandpa _____ me to study.
   a. stitched   b. encouraged   c. carved

5. Carole has a vivid _____ .
   a. series   b. originality   c. imagination

Name _____ Date _____

Activity 32

monuments	encouraged	series	mood	originality
local	period	biography	imagination	style

Write the word from the word box that matches each definition below.

1. _____ things built to honor a person or event

2. _____ newness

3. _____ a general state of mind

4. _____ a true story of someone's life written by another person

5. _____ several in a row

6. _____ in a nearby place

7. _____ urged someone to do something

8. _____ the way something is done

9. _____ a portion of time

10. _____ the ability to create new ideas in one's mind

UNIT 3 Imagination • **Lesson 5** *The Emperor's New Clothes*

Activity 33

---

emperor (p. 250) A ruler of an empire

vast (p. 251) Very large

scholars (p. 251) Plural of **scholar:** a person who has learned a great deal about a subject

occasion (p. 251) An event

unfit (p. 253) Not worthy

post (p. 253) A position that one is appointed to

weavers (p. 253) Plural of **weaver:** someone who makes something by passing strands of material over and under one another

looms (p. 254) Plural of **loom:** a machine for weaving thread into cloth

scarcely (p. 256) Barely

extraordinary (p. 257) Special

Fill in each blank with a vocabulary word from this lesson to complete each sentence.

1. The _____ used _____ to make colorful fabrics.

2. The farm covers a _____ area.

3. My ripped sweater is _____ for school.

4. Lyndsay _____ knows the new teacher.

5. Great Grandma's 100th birthday will be an _____

   _____ .

6. The _____ of ancient Rome was powerful.

UNIT 3 Imagination • **Lesson 5** *The Emperor's New Clothes*

Activity 34

Circle the word in parentheses that best fits each sentence.

1. It took Nancy a while to run across the (vast/sturdy) area.

2. The women were taking fabric off of the (scholars/looms).

3. We (promptly/scarcely) had time to eat lunch.

4. The (scholars/monuments) meet in the library.

5. The old, torn photograph is (unfit/scarely) to save.

6. I asked the (looms/weavers) about the rug.

7. Gregory was named to the (post/emperor) of ambassador.

8. Felicity wore her best dress for the (occasion/post).

9. Miles made an (unfit/extraordinary) dinner for me.

10. The (emperor/monuments) lived in a huge castle.

UNIT 3 Imagination • **Lesson 6** *Roxaboxen*

Activity 35

> **cactus** (p. 260) A desert plant
> **thorny** (p. 260) Full of thorns
> **plain** (p. 262) Not fancy
> **pottery** (p. 262) Objects that
>   are shaped from moist clay
>   and hardened by heat
> **mayor** (p. 262) The chief
>   elected official of a city
>
> **desert** (p. 263) Very dry land
> **bandits** (p. 265) Plural of
>   **bandit:** a robber
> **raids** (p. 265) Plural of **raid:** a
>   sudden attack
> **fierce** (p. 265) Wild
> **bordering** (p. 267) To touch at
>   the edge or boundary

**Review the vocabulary words and definitions
from *Roxaboxen*. Write two sentences that
each use at least one of the vocabulary words
from this lesson.**

1. _____

    _____

2. _____

    _____

UNIT 3 Imagination • **Lesson 6** *Roxaboxen*

Match each word on the left to its definition on the right.

1. plain   **a.** full of thorns

2. bandits   **b.** to touch at the edge or boundary

3. cactus   **c.** the chief elected official of a city

4. thorny   **d.** sudden attacks

5. raids   **e.** not fancy

6. mayor   **f.** a desert plant

7. pottery   **g.** wild

8. bordering   **h.** robbers

9. fierce   **i.** very dry land

10. desert   **j.** objects that are shaped from moist clay and hardened by heat

UNIT 3 Imagination • Review

Unit 3 Review

ordered	sturdy	monuments	spare
mood	practical	fierce	

Write the word from the word box that best matches the underlined word or phrase in the sentences below.

1. Layla visited the <u>things built to honor a person or event</u> in Washington, D.C. _____

2. Everyone at the party was in a happy <u>general state of mind</u>. _____

3. Rico placed the books on the <u>strong</u> bookshelves. _____

4. The <u>wild</u> lion roared loudly. _____

5. Marissa <u>asked for</u> an apple pie from the bakery.

   _____

6. You should always keep <u>extra</u> change in your pocket. _____

7. Heavy clothes are not <u>useful</u> on a hot sunny day. _____

Name _____ Date _____

Unit 3 Review

**Match each word on the left to its definition
on the right.**

1. imitating
2. vast
3. sculpture
4. straight away
5. scholars
6. carved
7. colonel
8. local
9. gutter
10. boxed

a. right now

b. an officer in the army,
marines, or air force

c. very large

d. people who have learned a
great deal about a subject

e. hit with the fist

f. copying

g. cut carefully

h. a figure, statue, or design
carved out of something solid

i. in a nearby place

j. a pipe that carries rainwater

UNIT 4 Money • **Lesson I** *A New Coat for Anna*

Activity 37

> **fuzzy** (p. 14) Having a lot of fur
> **remained** (p. 14) Past tense of **remain:** to stay
> **hardly** (p. 14) Not very much
> **spinning wheel** (p. 17) A machine used to make thread
> **yarn** (p. 17) A thread of twisted fibers
> **dye** (p. 18) A substance used to color materials
>
> **wound** (p. 19) Past tense of **wind:** to wrap around and around
> **measurements** (p. 20) Plural of **measurement:** the size of something
> **twirled** (p. 22) Past tense of **twirl:** to spin around quickly
> **reflection** (p. 22) An image seen in a surface such as water or glass

Circle the word in parentheses that best fits each sentence.

1. Jackson (remained/wound) inside during the ice storm.

2. I remember the (yarn/measurements) of the window.

3. Kevin used the (spinning wheel/reflection) to make yarn.

4. The socks were (fuzzy/twirled) and warm.

5. The (reflection/yarn) in my hat is bright red.

6. Kasey (wound/remained) the scarf around her head.

7. We (hardly/fuzzy) had time to eat our lunch.

8. The dancers (wound/twirled) around the floor.

Activity 38

twirled	wound	spinning wheel	yarn	reflection
measurements	hardly	remained	dye	fuzzy

Write the word from the word box that matches each definition below.

1. _____ stayed

2. _____ an image seen in a surface such as water or glass

3. _____ not very much

4. _____ a thread of twisted fibers

5. _____ a machine used to make thread

6. _____ a substance used to color materials

7. _____ spun around quickly

8. _____ having a lot of fur

9. _____ the size of something

10. _____ wrapped around and around

UNIT 4 Money • **Lesson 2** *Alexander, Who Used to Be Rich Last Sunday*

Activity 39

> **tokens** (p. 26) Plural of **token:** a piece of metal shaped like a coin, used instead of money
> **absolutely** (p. 29) Certainly
> **positively** (p. 29) Without a doubt
> **rent** (p. 29) To provide the use of something for a fee
>
> **rescued** (p. 31) Past tense of **rescue:** to save from danger
> **vanish** (p. 31) To disappear
> **non-returnable** (p. 33) Something that cannot be taken or given back

Review the vocabulary words and definitions from *Alexander, Who Used to Be Rich Last Sunday.* Write two sentences that each use at least one of the vocabulary words from this lesson.

1. _____

   _____

2. _____

   _____

Name _____ Date _____

Activity 40

| rent | non-returnable | vanish | rescued |
| positively | absolutely | tokens | |

Choose the word from the word box that best matches the underlined word or phrase in the sentences below.

1. Jenny <u>certainly</u> loves her little brother. _____

2. The bear <u>saved from danger</u> the cub from the wolf.

   _____

3. We <u>provide for a fee the use of</u> our cabin to other

   families. _____

4. Brian has <u>pieces of metal used instead of money</u> left

   from the county fair. _____

5. The clouds <u>disappear</u> when the sun comes out.

   _____

6. Renee is <u>without a doubt</u> the best soccer player.

   _____

7. The airplane tickets are <u>not able to be taken back</u>.

   _____

UNIT 4 Money • **Lesson 3** *Kids Did It! in Business*

Activity 41

---

track (p. 39) To follow the trail of

educational (p. 39) Helping one gain knowledge or a skill

profitable (p. 40) Making money

merchandise (p. 40) Items to be bought or sold

challenging (p. 40) Something requiring hard work and effort

donates (p. 42) Gives

profits (p. 42) Plural of **profit:** a gain in money

charity (p. 42) A group that gives help to the needy and operates without making any money

gadget (p. 44) A small, useful tool or device

widely (p. 44) Over a large area

Fill in each blank with a vocabulary word from this lesson to complete each sentence.

1. The family _____ old clothes to a

   _____ .

2. Jenna has a _____ catering business.

3. Tito worked for hours on the _____ homework.

4. Vickie used the _____ to buy more

   _____ .

5. We watched an _____ show about oceans.

6. Mom bought a _____ at the hardware store.

UNIT 4 Money • **Lesson 3** *Kids Did It! in Business*

Activity 42

Tell whether the boldfaced definition that is given for the underlined word in each sentence below makes sense. Circle Yes or No.

1. Chase <u>donates</u> money to help endangered animals.
   gives.. Yes   No

2. We used the <u>profits</u> from the garage sale for food.
   a gain in money.. Yes   No

3. The puppies <u>track</u> the smell of food.
   to follow the trail of...................................... Yes   No

4. My grandmother reads <u>educational</u> books.
   over a large area.. Yes   No

5. The <u>charity</u> had a party to raise money.
   something requiring hard work and effort....... Yes   No

6. I found a strange <u>gadget</u> in the garage.
   a small, useful tool or device....................... Yes   No

7. The flowers grew <u>widely</u> in the field.
   helping one to gain knowledge or skill .... Yes   No

8. The store has all new <u>merchandise</u>.
   items to be bought or sold............................. Yes   No

9. Carly read a long and <u>challenging</u> book.
   something requiring hard work and effort....... Yes   No

10. The team had a <u>profitable</u> bake sale.
    making money.. Yes   No

UNIT 4 Money • **Lesson 4** *The Cobbler's Song*

Activity 43

> **cobbler** (p. 48) A person who repairs shoes and boots
> **mended** (p. 48) Past tense of **mend**: to fix or repair
> **dreadful** (p. 49) Terrible
> **recognizing** (p. 49) Knowing someone
>
> **workbench** (p. 51) A strong table used for working with tools and materials
> **glared** (p. 52) Past tense of **glare**: to give an angry look
> **pale** (p. 53) Light in color
> **relieved** (p. 53) Past tense of **relieve**: to comfort

Circle the correct word that completes each sentence.

1. The rotten eggs had a _____ smell.
   a. relieved   b. dreadful   c. pale

2. Abby _____ her old jacket.
   a. glared   b. twirled   c. mended

3. I wore a _____ shirt with my black pants.
   a. profitable   b. challenging   c. pale

4. Darice _____ when the car honked.
   a. mended   b. rescued   c. glared

5. Randi is _____ the boy from school.
   a. recognizing   b. glared   c. relieved

6. Dalton fixed the toy on the _____ .
   a. merchandise   b. workbench   c. gadget

UNIT 4 Money • **Lesson 4** *The Cobbler's Song*

Activity 44

Match each word on the left to its definition on the right.

1. pale

a. gave an angry look

2. relieved

b. fixed or repaired

3. dreadful

c. light in color

4. cobbler

d. a strong table used for working with tools and materials

5. recognizing

e. a person who repairs shoes and boots

6. glared

f. terrible

7. mended

g. knowing someone

8. workbench

h. comforted

UNIT 4 Money • **Lesson 5** *Four Dollars and Fifty Cents*

Activity 45

> **bills** (p. 58) Plural of **bill**: a notice of money owed
> **collecting** (p. 58) Getting money
> **suspicions** (p. 60) Plural of **suspicion**: a feeling of doubt
> **volunteered** (p. 61) Past tense of **volunteer**: to offer to do something
> **graze** (p. 61) To eat grass
>
> **determined** (p. 62) Firm and unwilling to change
> **lugged** (p. 64) Past tense of **lug**: to drag
> **padlock** (p. 65) A heavy lock
> **clenched** (p. 67) Past tense of **clench**: to close tightly
> **hollered** (p. 68) Past tense of **holler**: to call out loudly

**Fill in each blank with a vocabulary word
from this lesson to complete each sentence.**

1. Shannon is _____ to do well on her science test.

2. Owen _____ to clean on his mother's birthday.

3. We _____ all of the books to the new library.

4. Kelsey put a _____ on the garage door.

5. I have _____ about the new coach.

6. The sheep _____ behind the barn.

7. I will pay my _____ when I get my paycheck tomorrow.

8. My jaw _____ when I heard the loud thunder.

Activity 46

lugged	hollered	padlock	collecting	graze
volunteered	bills	clenched	suspicions	determined

Write the word from the word box that matches each definition below.

1. _____ closed tightly

2. _____ a heavy lock

3. _____ feelings of doubt

4. _____ getting money

5. _____ firm and unwilling to change

6. _____ notices of money owed

7. _____ dragged

8. _____ to eat grass

9. _____ called out loudly

10. _____ offered to do something

UNIT 4 Money • **Lesson 6** *The Go-Around Dollar*

Activity 47

> **presses** (p. 72) Plural of **press:** a printing machine
> **seal** (p. 72) An official stamp
> **portrait** (p. 74) A picture of someone
> **debts** (p. 76) Plural of **debt:** something that is owed to another
> **formula** (p. 80) A set method for doing something
>
> **counterfeit** (p. 80) Fake
> **emblem** (p. 85) A sign or figure that stands for something
> **official** (p. 87) A person who holds a certain office or position
> **remains** (p. 87) What is left
> **inspect** (p. 87) To look at closely

Review the vocabulary words and definitions from *The Go-Around Dollar*. Write two sentences that each use at least one of the vocabulary words from this lesson.

1. _____

   _____

2. _____

   _____

UNIT 4 Money • **Lesson 6** *The Go-Around Dollar*

Circle the word in parentheses that best fits each sentence.

1. We watched the (presses/debts) print the dollar bills.

2. The team (formula/emblem) is on the school sign.

3. Aaron knew the dollar was (dreadful/counterfeit) by the color.

4. I paid the (debts/remains) with my mowing money.

5. The (cobbler/official) said the building was closed.

6. I spilled the (remains/bills) of my chocolate milk.

7. John Singer Sargent painted the (formula/portrait) *Miss Eleanor Brooks.*

8. The (reflection/seal) of the county is on the courthouse door.

9. Liam and Whitney (inspect/rent) the packages.

10. We learned a (formula/counterfeit) to solve the problem.

UNIT 4 Money • **Lesson 7** *Uncle Jed's Barbershop*

Activity 49

> **county** (p. 94) Part of a state
> **equipment** (p. 95) Tools and supplies used for a given purpose
> **exchange** (p. 96) To trade one thing for another
> **segregation** (p. 97) The practice of setting one group apart from another
> **unconscious** (p. 97) Not awake
> **examine** (p. 97) To look at in detail
>
> **bundled** (p. 98) Past tense of **bundle:** to wrap together
> **failing** (p. 100) Losing worth
> **disappointed** (p. 100) Past tense of **disappoint:** unhappy that something expected did not occur
> **stations** (p. 102) Plural of **station:** a place where a service is performed

Circle the correct word that completes each sentence.

1. Kurt _____ the baby in a blanket.
   a. bundled   b. lugged   c. disappointed

2. We _____ our report cards carefully.
   a. exchange   b. graze   c. examine

3. Alexis is _____ that she can't go with us.
   a. disappointed   b. unconscious   c. pale

4. Josh was _____ after he fell.
   a. unconscious   b. bundled   c. dreadful

5. Damian and Colin _____ shoes in gym.
   a. inspect   b. examine   c. exchange

Name _____ Date _____

UNIT 4 Money • **Lesson 7** *Uncle Jed's Barbershop*

Activity 50

Match each word on the left to its definition on the right.

1. exchange

2. equipment

3. failing

4. unconscious

5. bundled

6. stations

7. segregation

8. disappointed

9. county

10. examine

a. wrapped together

b. places where a service is performed

c. not awake

d. losing worth

e. tools and supplies used for a given purpose

f. to trade one thing for another

g. to look at in detail

h. part of a state

i. unhappy that something expected did not occur

j. the practice of setting one group apart from another

Unit 4 Review

Circle the word in parentheses that best fits each sentence.

1. The leaves (hollered/twirled) in the wind.

2. Gretchen used (bills/dye) to color the cloth.

3. The (cobbler/county) sewed the hole in my boot.

4. My mom was (clenched/relieved) when she received a good report from the doctor.

5. The volunteer was (recognizing/collecting) money for charity.

6. The team picked up the (equipment/portrait) after the game.

7. Ali drove the car to the (station/cobbler) to be fixed.

8. The young girl smiled at her (official/reflection) in the mirror.

9. Josh and Miguel (rescued/hollered) as they rode the roller coaster.

10. We (hardly/widely) know our neighbors.

UNIT 4 Money • Review

Unit 4 Review

widely	track	portrait	segregation	bills
clenched	rescued	county	inspect	official

Write the word from the word box that matches each definition below.

1. _____ part of a state

2. _____ notices of money owed

3. _____ over a large area

4. _____ to look at closely

5. _____ a picture of someone

6. _____ the practice of setting one group apart from another

7. _____ a person who holds a certain office or position

8. _____ to follow the trail of

9. _____ closed tightly

10. _____ saved from danger

UNIT 5 Storytelling • **Lesson I** *A Story A Story*

Activity 5l

defenseless (p. 108) Helpless
outwit (p. 108) To be more
   clever than
phrases (p. 108) Plural of
   phrase: a part of a sentence
merely (p. 110) Simply
bind (p. 110) To tie together
tatter (p. 111) To tear
furious (p. 113) Violently angry

captives (p. 114) Plural of
   captive: a prisoner
praise (p. 115) Words that
   show high regard and
   approval
assembled (p. 115) Past
   tense of **assemble:** to come
   together

**Write the vocabulary word from this lesson
that best matches the underlined word or
phrase in the sentences below.**

1. The whole class <u>came together</u> on the playground.

   _____

2. Did you <u>tie together</u> the sticks of wood? _____

3. The mouse was <u>helpless</u> against the cat. _____

4. Don't <u>tear</u> your shirt on the broken chair. _____

5. The teacher read the <u>parts of the sentence</u> slowly.

   _____

UNIT 5 Storytelling • **Lesson I** *A Story A Story*

defenseless	captives	bind	furious	phrases
praise	outwit	tatter	merely	assembled

Write the word from the word box that completes each sentence.

1. Can the students _____ the teacher?

2. Amara _____ asked to go home.

3. We hope that the _____ will be freed soon.

4. Reggie will _____ the box together with yarn.

5. The family _____ to play a game.

6. Andy helped the _____ baby.

7. George was _____ that we ate his dinner.

8. How did you _____ your football shirt?

9. My teacher gave me _____ for the

_____ I wrote.

UNIT 5 **Storytelling • Lesson 2** *Oral History*

Activity 53

> **ancestors** (p. 120) Plural of **ancestor:** a parent, grandparent, great-grandparent, and so on
>
> **ancient** (p. 120) Very old
>
> **recited** (p. 120) Past tense of **recite:** to tell aloud
>
> **deeds** (p. 120) Plural of **deed:** an act
>
> **oral** (p. 120) Spoken
>
> **inherited** (p. 121) Past tense of **inherit:** to receive another person's property after his or her death
>
> **folklore** (p. 122) The legends, beliefs, and customs of a group of people
>
> **traditional** (p. 122) Commonly practiced, used, or encountered
>
> **published** (p. 122) Past tense of **publish:** to print
>
> **series** (p. 122) Several in a row

Circle the word in parentheses that best fits each sentence.

1. My (deeds/ancestors) came from Africa.

2. Teri (recited/inherited) a poem for the class.

3. I can't read the (ancient/series) letters.

4. Jaime learned the (oral/traditional) way to cook.

5. Our teacher (inherited/published) the class newspaper.

6. Mario is learning the (folklore/ancestors) of Russia.

Name _____ Date _____

Activity 54

deeds	ancient	published	series	traditional
folklore	ancestors	recited	inherited	oral

Write the word from the word box that matches each definition below.

1. _____ commonly practiced, used, or encountered

2. _____ printed

3. _____ spoken

4. _____ acts

5. _____ several in a row

6. _____ very old

7. _____ the legends, beliefs, and customs of a group of people

8. _____ parents, grandparents, great-grandparents, and so on

9. _____ told aloud

10. _____ received another person's property after his or her death

Activity 55

---

streaming (p. 128) Running
faucet (p. 131) A water tap
mantel (p. 132) A shelf above a
  fireplace
siren (p. 132) A device that
  makes a loud, shrill sound
scarcely (p. 134) Barely
drenched (p. 134) Past tense of
  drench: to soak completely

brave (p. 136) Having courage
errand (p. 136) A short trip to
  do something
overcome (p. 140) To beat or
  conquer
natural (p. 141) Not artificial
  or made by humans

**Review the vocabulary words and definitions
from *Storm in the Night*. Write two sentences
that each use at least one of the vocabulary
words from this lesson.**

1. _____

   _____

2. _____

   _____

UNIT 5 Storytelling • **Lesson 3** *Storm in the Night*

Activity 56

Tell whether the boldfaced definition that is given for the underlined word in each sentence below makes sense. Circle Yes or No.

1. The <u>faucet</u> drips all night long.
   a water tap .... Yes   No

2. Cameron went on an <u>errand</u> with his mom.
   a short trip to do something................. Yes   No

3. The heavy rains <u>drenched</u> my clothes.
   soaked completely................................... Yes   No

4. I put my hat on the <u>mantel</u> to dry.
   a water tap .... Yes   No

5. The tired runner couldn't <u>overcome</u> the other
   runners.   **to beat or conquer**................... Yes   No

6. June is <u>brave</u> to go outside in the dark.
   not artificial or made by humans........ Yes   No

7. The tears were <u>streaming</u> down Lara's face.
   running .... Yes   No

8. A police <u>siren</u> woke me up this morning.
   a device that makes a loud, shrill sound .... Yes   No

9. <u>Natural</u> rock formations overlook the river.
   running .... Yes   No

10. Perry <u>scarcely</u> woke up in time for school.
    barely.. Yes   No

UNIT 5 **Storytelling • Lesson 4** *Carving the Pole*

Activity 57

> **symbol** (p. 146) Something that stands for something else
> **reservation** (p. 146) Land that is set aside for the use of Native American tribes
> **skill** (p. 146) The ability to do something
> **legends** (p. 146) Plural of **legend:** a story passed down that is not entirely true
> **knot** (p. 147) A hard, dark place in wood
>
> **common** (p. 147) Often found
> **transfers** (p. 148) Moves
> **represents** (p. 149) Stands for
> **storage** (p. 151) A place for keeping things
> **traditions** (p. 152) Plural of **tradition:** a custom handed down through many generations

Circle the correct word that completes each sentence.

1. I like the Native American _____ about animals.
   a. phrases   b. knots   c. legends

2. Ian has _____ in singing.
   a. traditions   b. skill   c. legends

3. Gabriela put her sweaters in _____ .
   a. symbol   b. storage   c. knot

4. Pine trees are _____ in Canada.
   a. common   b. defenseless   c. brave

5. Kira drew the _____ for peace.
   a. knot   b. symbol   c. reservation

UNIT 5 Storytelling • **Lesson 4** *Carving the Pole*

Activity 58

**Match each word on the left to its definition
on the right.**

1. knot

2. legends

3. traditions

4. symbol

5. skill

6. reservation

7. represents

8. storage

9. transfers

10. common

a. land that is set aside for the
   use of Native American tribes

b. moves

c. stands for

d. the ability to do something

e. a hard, dark place in wood

f. something that stands for
   something else

g. often found

h. a place for keeping things

i. stories passed down that are
   not entirely true

j. customs handed down
   through many generations

UNIT 5 Storytelling • **Lesson 5** *The Keeping Quilt*

Activity 59

> **quilt** (p. 158) A bedcovering
> made of two pieces of cloth
> and stuffed with soft material
> **hauling** (p. 158) Carrying
> **artificial** (p. 158) Made by
> people rather than nature
>
> **scraps** (p. 159) Plural of **scrap:**
> a small piece
> **border** (p. 159) A strip along
> the edge of something
> **flavor** (p. 161) Taste

**Write the vocabulary word from this lesson
that best matches the underlined word or
phrase in the sentences below.**

1. The <u>strip along the edge</u> of the blanket was

   purple. _____

2. Jordy used <u>small pieces</u> of wood to make a box.

   _____

3. The <u>taste</u> of lemons is sour.

   _____

4. The flowers on the table look <u>made by people</u>

   <u>rather than nature</u>. _____

5. My brothers are <u>carrying</u> out the trash.

   _____

Name _____ Date _____

hauling	border	artificial
quilt	scraps	flavor

Write the word from the word box that completes each sentence.

1. I will use _____ from old clothes to make a

   _____ .

2. Grape gum has a(n) _____ taste.

3. Tuan drew animals on the _____ of the paper.

4. Delia loves the _____ of spinach.

5. The teachers are _____ their books to the cars.

UNIT 5 Storytelling • **Lesson 6** *Johnny Appleseed*

Activity 61

stored (p. 169) Past tense of **store:** to put away for future use

cleared (p. 169) Past tense of **clear:** to remove things from

survived (p. 170) Past tense of **survive:** to stay alive

boasted (p. 171) Past tense of **boast:** to brag

exhausted (p. 171) Tired

affectionately (p. 172) With love

exaggerated (p. 174) Past tense of **exaggerate:** to go beyond the truth

recalled (p. 174) Past tense of **recall:** to remember

certain (p. 176) Sure

claim (p. 177) To say that something is true

Circle the word in parentheses that best fits each sentence.

1. Kurt (cleared/recalled) the dishes from the table.

2. Sofia (stored/boasted) about her good grades.

3. Ken is (certain/affectionately) he will win.

4. The birds (survived/exaggerated) the huge storm.

5. We were (exhausted/cleared) after the long walk.

6. Jessica (recalled/stored) the blankets in the cedar chest.

7. Nick (survived/exaggerated) about the fish he caught.

Activity 62

survived	exaggerated	exhausted	claim	boasted
certain	stored	recalled	affectionately	cleared

**Write the word from the word box that
matches each definition below.**

1. _____ remembered

2. _____ to say that something is true

3. _____ removed things from

4. _____ tired

5. _____ sure

6. _____ stayed alive

7. _____ put away for future use

8. _____ bragged

9. _____ with love

10. _____ went beyond the truth

Activity 63

> **memories** (p. 180) Plural of **memory:** a thing or time remembered
>
> **straw** (p. 186) Dried grain stalks
>
> **rescue** (p. 188) To save from danger
>
> **rippled** (p. 188) Past tense of **ripple:** to make a very small wave
>
> **fetch** (p. 189) To go after and bring back

Review the vocabulary words and definitions from *Aunt Flossie's Hats*. Write two sentences that each use at least one of the vocabulary words from this lesson.

1. _____

   _____

2. _____

   _____

UNIT 5 Storytelling • **Lesson 7** *Aunt Flossie's Hats*

Activity 64

straw	fetch	memories
rippled	rescue	

Write the word from the word box that completes each sentence.

1. The water _____ over the rocks.

2. Bill put fresh _____ in the barn.

3. Granddad has happy _____ of his childhood.

4. Noelle and Cindy _____ stray cats.

5. Our dog likes to _____ the newspaper.

Unit 5 Review

Circle the correct word that completes each sentence.

1. My grandfather shares _____ stories about his childhood.
   a. series   b. oral   c. inherited

2. There is a _____ in the top of the table.
   a. knot   b. claim   c. mantel

3. Many people live on the _____ .
   a. reservation   b. knot   c. memories

4. Anne acted in a _____ of plays.
   a. deeds   b. transfer   c. series

5. Mom _____ calls me Sweetie.
   a. scarcely   b. affectionately   c. exaggerated

6. Brad _____ books from the classroom to the library.
   a. transfers   b. represents   c. captives

7. My parents _____ that fish is good for you.
   a. outwit   b. exaggerated   c. claim

8. Dorie _____ the answer to the math question.
   a. recalled   b. inherited   c. drenched

9. Cameron _____ his grandfather's piano.
   a. published   b. assembled   c. inherited

10. The plus sign _____ addition in math.
    a. represents   b. transfers   c. series

Name _____ Date _____

Unit 5 Review

captives	outwit	memories	furious	merely
deeds	drenched	scarcely	exaggerated	streaming

Write the word from the word box that matches each definition below.

1. _____ soaked completely

2. _____ simply

3. _____ went beyond the truth

4. _____ violently angry

5. _____ running

6. _____ to be more clever than

7. _____ acts

8. _____ barely

9. _____ prisoners

10. _____ things or times remembered

Activity 65

> **plain** (p. 198) Not fancy
> **sensible** (p. 198) Having or showing good sense
> **quantity** (p. 198) A number or amount
> **quality** (p. 198) Degree of excellence
> **dullness** (p. 199) State of being boring
>
> **manner** (p. 200) The way in which something is done
> **crimson** (p. 200) Deep red
> **splendid** (p. 200) Magnificent
> **hostess** (p. 200) A woman who receives or entertains guests
> **scurried** (p. 201) Past tense of **scurry:** to move quickly

Fill in each blank with a vocabulary word from this lesson to complete each sentence.

1. What is the _____ of oranges in this bag?

2. Doug is very _____ about his homework.

3. Patrice _____ to the front of the line.

4. My _____ of talking is slow.

5. The _____ hat did not match the orange coat.

6. Did you see the _____ sunset last night?

7. Ashley baked a high _____ cake.

8. Kayla wore her _____ red dress to the dance.

UNIT 6 Country Life • **Lesson I** *The Country Mouse and the City Mouse*

Activity 66

**Match each word on the left to its definition
on the right.**

1. quantity

    a. the way in which something is done

2. sensible

    b. moved quickly

3. splendid

    c. a woman who receives or entertains guests

4. manner

    d. having or showing good sense

5. scurried

    e. degree of excellence

6. dullness

    f. a number or amount

7. plain

    g. magnificent

8. crimson

    h. state of being boring

9. hostess

    i. not fancy

10. quality

    j. deep red

UNIT 6 Country Life • **Lesson 2** *Heartland*

Activity 67

> **silos** (p. 204) Plural of **silo:** a
> tall building for storing food
> for animals
> **fertile** (p. 204) Fruitful
> **bred** (p. 206) Past tense of
> **breed:** to raise plants or
> animals
> **define** (p. 207) To describe
>
> **analyze** (p. 207) To examine
> **vital** (p. 208) Necessary
> **descends** (p. 209) Comes down
> **drought** (p. 210) Dry weather
> that lasts a very long time
> **reigns** (p. 210) Rules
> **possess** (p. 211) To have

**Tell whether the boldfaced definition that
is given for the underlined word in each
sentence below makes sense. Circle Yes
or No.**

1. The farmer bred unusual chickens.
   described .... Yes   No

2. The rain is vital to the plants.
   necessary .... Yes   No

3. The queen reigns over the whole country.
   rules .... Yes   No

4. The drought is killing the corn.
   a tall building for storing food for animals........ Yes   No

5. The doctors analyze the sick children.
   to examine .... Yes   No

UNIT 6 Country Life • **Lesson 2** *Heartland*

Activity 68

Circle the word in parentheses that best fits each sentence.

1. Daria (descends/reigns) the stairs to the basement.

2. Mom (reigns/vital) over our family.

3. I have to (drought/define) ten words for science class.

4. Imelda is (vital/plain) to the committee.

5. If the (drought/manner) ends, the soil will be (sensible/fertile).

6. The (reigns/silos) are full of corn.

7. Reva (scurried/bred) sheep last year.

8. Brent and Gina (possess/descends) a key to the house.

9. Did you (possess/analyze) the soil for insects?

Name _____   Date _____

UNIT 6 **Country Life • Lesson 3** *Leah's Pony*

Activity 69

swift (p. 216) Able to move quickly

glistened (p. 217) Past tense of glisten: to sparkle

eager (p. 222) Filled with excitement or interest

gullies (p. 223) Plural of gully: a narrow ditch made by flowing water

clustered (p. 224) Past tense of cluster: to gather together

clutched (p. 224) Past tense of clutch: to hold tightly

fertilize (p. 224) To add a substance to soil to make it better for growing crops

cultivate (p. 224) To help plants grow better by breaking up the soil around them

practically (p. 226) Almost

supposed (p. 228) Past tense of suppose: to expect

Circle the correct word that completes each sentence.

1. The water _____ on the leaves.
   a. scurried   b. clutched   c. glistened

2. Ariana _____ her teddy bear.
   a. clutched   b. supposed   c. scurried

3. The _____ deer ran into the woods.
   a. swift   b. crimson   c. eager

4. Diego is _____ to drive the tractor.
   a. swift   b. eager   c. splendid

5. Mia _____ the weeds in a pile.
   a. glistened   b. clutched   c. clustered

UNIT 6 Country Life • **Lesson 3** *Leah's Pony*

Activity 70

clustered	gullies	fertilize	supposed	practically
glistened	eager	cultivate	clutched	swift

**Write the word from the word box that
matches each definition below.**

1. _____ filled with excitement or interest

2. _____ narrow ditches made by flowing water

3. _____ to help plants grow better by breaking up
   the soil around them

4. _____ almost

5. _____ held tightly

6. _____ sparkled

7. _____ to add a substance to soil to make it better
   for growing crops

8. _____ able to move quickly

9. _____ expected

10. _____ gathered together

Activity 71

---

pastures (p. 236) Plural of
  pasture: a piece of land on
  which animals graze
bales (p. 239) Plural of **bale:** A
  large bundle of hay
firm (p. 242) Solid
automatic (p. 242) Operating
  by itself

suction (p. 242) A pulling force
  that uses a sucking action
cartons (p. 243) Plural of
  carton: a container that is
  made of cardboard, paper, or
  other material

**Review the vocabulary words and definitions
from *Cows in the Parlor*. Write two sentences
that each use at least one of the vocabulary
words from this lesson.**

1. _____

   _____

2. _____

   _____

UNIT 6 Country Life • **Lesson 4** *Cows in the Parlor*

Activity 72

firm	cartons	suction
automatic	bales	pastures

Choose the word from the word box that best matches the underlined word or phrase in the sentences below.

1. The <u>lands on which animals graze</u> were green and wet.

   _____

2. Dustin put the <u>containers made of cardboard</u> on the bus.

   _____

3. Dad uses <u>a pulling force that uses a sucking action</u> to empty the

   tank.   _____

4. Todd buys <u>large bundles of hay</u> from the big farm down the road.

   _____

5. The ground is <u>solid</u> and dry.   _____

6. The heater is <u>operating by itself</u> and turns on at night.

   _____

UNIT 6 **Country Life • Lesson 5** *Just Plain Fancy*

Activity 73

> **reins** (p. 250) Plural of **rein:** a strap used to guide and control a horse
>
> **responsibility** (p. 251) A duty
>
> **unusual** (p. 251) Not common
>
> **nestled** (p. 251) Past tense of **nestle:** to settle safely
>
> **eased** (p. 252) Past tense of **ease:** to move carefully
>
> **constantly** (p. 253) All the time
>
> **folk** (p. 255) People
>
> **shamed** (p. 255) Past tense of **shame:** to disgrace
>
> **authority** (p. 255) The power to make decisions, command, or control
>
> **darted** (p. 257) Past tense of **dart:** to move suddenly and quickly

Fill in each blank with a vocabulary word from this lesson to complete each sentence.

1. The horse _____ into the warm straw.

2. The rabbit _____ into the hole.

3. Liza took the _____ of the horse

4. We saw an _____ bird at the zoo.

5. Jesse _____ into the quiet room.

6. I have a _____ to cut the grass.

7. Curtis has the _____ to put us to work.

UNIT 6 Country Life • **Lesson 5** *Just Plain Fancy*

| responsibility | authority | nestled | folk | unusual |
| eased | shamed | darted | constantly | reins |

Write the word from the word box that matches each definition below.

1. _____ disgraced

2. _____ the power to make decisions, command, or control

3. _____ moved suddenly and quickly

4. _____ straps used to guide and control a horse

5. _____ all the time

6. _____ people

7. _____ a duty

8. _____ settled safely

9. _____ not common

10. _____ moved carefully

Activity 75

> **seasonal** (p. 269) Ripe at a
>   certain time
> **produce** (p. 269) Farm
>   products, such as fresh fruits
>   and vegetables
> **particular** (p. 269) Special
> **necessities** (p. 272) Plural of
>   **necessity:** something that is
>   needed
> **elevated** (p. 275) Past tense of
>   **elevate:** to raise up
>
> **installed** (p. 275) Past tense of
>   **install:** to put in place for use
>   or service
> **featuring** (p. 279) Having as
>   the main attraction
> **discount** (p. 279) With lower
>   prices
> **expire** (p. 280) To come to an
>   end
> **dividers** (p. 280) Plural of
>   **divider:** anything that cuts a
>   thing into parts

**Circle the word in parentheses that best fits
each sentence.**

1. Rashir (shamed/installed) the new lights.

2. Bernie found (discount/fertile) tools to buy.

3. Mom buys (produce/reins) every Saturday.

4. I put (cartons/dividers) into my big notebook.

5. Maggie is searching for a (particular/swift) book.

6. We went to a concert (featuring/practically) my
   favorite singer.

7. Bailey took only the (reins/necessities) with her.

UNIT 6 Country Life • **Lesson 6** *Whatever Happened to the Baxter Place?*

Activity 76

Match each word on the left to its definition on the right.

1. featuring

    a. farm products, such as fresh fruits and vegetables

2. particular

    b. special

3. dividers

    c. to come to an end

4. produce

    d. with lower prices

5. installed

    e. things that are needed

6. seasonal

    f. raised up

7. elevated

    g. things that cut something into parts

8. discount

    h. ripe at a certain time

9. expire

    i. put in place for use or service

10. necessities

    j. having as the main attraction

Activity 77

prairie (p. 284) Flat or rolling land covered with grass

dugouts (p. 284) Plural of **dugout:** a shelter made by digging a hole in the ground or on the side of a hill

core (p. 285) The central part of something

monstrous (p. 286) Huge

grains (p. 288) Plural of **grain:** a seed of corn, wheat, oats, rye, or another type of cereal plant

drifts (p. 289) Plural of **drift:** a mound formed by blowing wind

bitter (p. 291) Harsh

grit (p. 292) Very small bits of sand or stone

vast (p. 292) Very large

blazing (p. 293) Very hot

Review the vocabulary words and definitions from *If you're not from the prairie*. Write two sentences that each use at least one of the vocabulary words from this lesson.

1. _____

   _____

2. _____

   _____

UNIT 6 Country Life • **Lesson 7** *If you're not from the prairie*

Activity 78

Circle the correct word that completes each sentence.

1. A fire moved across the open _____ .
    a. drifts   b. prairie   c. gullies

2. The Burts plant _____ in their fields.
    a. grains   b. dugouts   c. bales

3. Farmers made _____ for shelter and storage.
    a. drifts   b. dugouts   c. produce

4. The students are the _____ of the school.
    a. grit   b. dividers   c. core

5. The _____ of snow hid the fences.
    a. drifts   b. bales   c. dugouts

6. Mark has a piece of _____ in his eye.
    a. produce   b. grit   c. core

7. The _____ sun burns the plants.
    a. blazing   b. seasonal   c. automatic

8. We found a _____ pile of trash.
    a. bitter   b. seasonal   c. monstrous

9. Jayne slowly crossed the _____ field.
    a. vast   b. grit   c. particular

10. A _____ wind blew through the windows.
    a. blazing   b. bitter   c. crimson

UNIT 6 Country Life • Review

Unit 6 Review

Circle the word in parentheses that best fits each sentence.

1. The (silos/hostess/folk) showed the guests to their table.

2. Sondra bought a (define/dullness/splendid) dress for the party.

3. It is (practically/constantly/featuring) summer.

4. The storm made (folk/gullies/silos) in the field.

5. Jason (shamed/elevated/supposed) his feet after work.

6. My library card will (expire/cultivate/analyze) this month.

7. The farm has a (seasonal/dullness/drought) crop of peaches.

8. The slow weekend was filled with (splendid/authority/dullness).

9. Marissa will (define/cultivate/expire) the dirt around the peas.

10. We are (shamed/practically/supposed) to visit my grandmother this weekend.

Vocabulary Activities

Name _____ Date _____

▶ Unit 6 Review

quality	featuring	descends	folk	authority
silos	constantly	drought	define	shamed

Write the word from the word box that matches each definition below.

1. _____ having as the main attraction

2. _____ degree of excellence

3. _____ comes down

4. _____ to describe

5. _____ disgraced

6. _____ the power to make decisions, command, or control

7. _____ people

8. _____ dry weather that lasts a very long time

9. _____ tall buildings for storing food for animals

10. _____ all the time